MAXIMISE MINDFULNESS
MINIMISE MINDLESSNESS

Sam Drake is a talented counsellor with many years of experience in the mental health industry. He is a member of the Australian Counselling Association. He has worked as a counsellor with adolescents, adults, and couples, and as a mental health public speaker, workplace trainer and mindfulness coach.

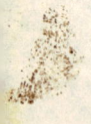

MAXIMISE MINDFULNESS
MINIMISE MINDLESSNESS

SAM DRAKE

Published by
Rupa Publications India Pvt. Ltd 2023
7/16, Ansari Road, Daryaganj
New Delhi 110002

Sales Centres:
Bengaluru Chennai
Hyderabad Jaipur Kathmandu
Kolkata Mumbai Prayagraj

Copyright © Sam Drake 2023

The views and opinions expressed in this book are the author's own and the facts are as reported by him which have been verified to the extent possible, and the publishers are not in any way liable for the same.

All rights reserved.
No part of this publication may be reproduced, transmitted, or stored in a retrieval system, in any form or by any means, electronic, mechanical, photocopying, recording or otherwise, without the prior permission of the publisher.

P-ISBN: 978-93-5702-131-9
E-ISBN: 978-93-5702-132-6

First impression 2023

10 9 8 7 6 5 4 3 2 1

Printed in India

This book is sold subject to the condition that it shall not, by way of trade or otherwise, be lent, resold, hired out, or otherwise circulated, without the publisher's prior consent, in any form of binding or cover other than that in which it is published.

For my mother, Gail.
The bravest, kindest and most inspiring person
I'll ever know

CONTENTS

Introduction — 9

1. What Mindfulness Is, and What It Is Not — 13
2. The Mindlessness Paradox — 19
3. How to Maximise Mindfulness and Minimise Mindlessness — 27
4. [Dope]amine — 34
5. The Do Nothing Approach to Mindfulness — 41
6. Getting Emotional — 45
7. Sensing our Senses — 55
8. Remembering to Breathe — 65

9. Gratitude & the Shoulda, Woulda, Couldas	72
10. Meditation: Myths and Misconceptions	79
11. Val-U-es	88
12. ProcrastiNation	102
13. The A Word	115
14. Final Thoughts	125

INTRODUCTION

Dear reader,

Thank you for investing your time (and money) into reading this book. Like all "self-help" books (I'd prefer to refer to as an aid), there will be material in here you will find interesting, pragmatic and useful. There may also be material you find too abstract, nonsensical, airy-fairy, or just plain awful. We are all unique and inherently complex beings—all I can ask is that you approach this book with an open-mind and an open-heart, and be authentic with yourself about what it is *you* want from this experience.

My first experience with mindfulness came at 20 years old. It was around the time that I was diagnosed with bipolar disorder, had a severe drug addiction, and was contemplating suicide. I was hoping, like so many do, that I would find my "magic pill"—the thing that would fix everything and send me hurtling into a new life with a new found appreciation for spirituality, an aversion to drugs, and a new-found confidence I had never before experienced!

I didn't.

I stormed out of the mindfulness meditation session I had attended, more disillusioned and angrier than ever. I called it "total bullshit"—an exercise and practice for those who didn't understand suffering, who had the perfect lives already manifested, who had the *opportunity* and *privilege* to engage in these practices, because they hadn't suffered like I had.

What I thought was a complete failure, however, eventually became the foundation for my desperately needed personal development.

Although I was disheartened initially, I didn't give up. As a lifelong underachiever and a quitter, this was huge for me. I went onto YouTube, I searched for a guided mindfulness exercise, and I found one with a voice I was attuned to. That was when my journey began.

Introduction

I sought therapy at the time also. The combination of my rehabilitation, therapy, and mindfulness training drove me to change. I began having 'AHA' moments frequently, such as "appreciate what ya got" and "if I want the world to be more empathic, but all I do is sit around, complain and don't actually *do* anything for others, then I'm a damn hypocrite!" Thanks to Gandhi for that—"be the change you want to see" stuck with me more than anything else at that time.

So, mindfulness and meditation weren't the "magic pill" I was looking for—but it created the opportunity to become more self-aware, which gave way to greater self-confidence, which eventually informed empathy and authenticity.

Everyone's journey with mindfulness is unique—you may find that you sleep a little better. You may find that you're more emotionally intelligent. You may find that it gives you a momentary reprieve from anger, or sadness, or that you are a little less stressed. There is no right or wrong. Whatever happens for you, happens. Take it all with a sense of gratitude, even if the reasons why you begin your mindfulness journey don't eventuate. I began mindfulness primarily to decrease bouts of anger, and yet that's the one thing I still struggle with! (Yes, road-rage is truly a plight).

We all have complicated issues, most of which are not our fault. We are almost *always* our worst enemies, but on the flip-side of that, we are also our *greatest* asset. It may sound harsh, but no-one is responsible for fixing our problems but ourselves. Others can offer support, constructive feedback, and even love—but we are the ones who will either be capable of facing our challenges and moving toward the top of the mountain—or be crushed by an avalanche.

Dear reader, it means so much to me for you investing your time to read this book, even if you only appreciate or remember 2% of it—I appreciate you. I'm so grateful for the fact that I had an opportunity to share something with you that I'm hopelessly and desperately passionate about. I hope you recognise by the end of this book that you have all of the internal resources necessary to incorporate mindfulness and decrease mindlessness. Mostly, I hope that this book aids you on your journey of meaning and purpose, and that you recognise the capacity to make change within yourself.

1
WHAT MINDFULNESS IS, AND WHAT IT IS NOT

Mindfulness—like anything pigeonholed as being a revivalist spiritual practice for new age hippies and the wealthy upper-class—is frequently misinterpreted, misunderstood, and misconceived. Consequently, many of us who consider ourselves as "regular folks" are turned off of the idea of learning this pragmatic skill; often because our preconceptions of mindfulness are that it is airy-fairy, hippy-dippy nonsense, deem it "too difficult" or "a total scam" because we didn't achieve instantaneous results from our first attempt at mindfulness—or, because it didn't magically fix all of our issues and send us hurtling back into life with a new-found appreciation for everything that does-or-could exist. I get it. I stormed out of my first mindfulness meditation session like a gorilla, huffing and puffing and mumbling about mindfulness being a scam.

So what *is* mindfulness, really?

Mindfulness basically translates to present moment awareness. It is a *quality* that is learnable, teachable, and cross-contextually applicable. At its core, mindfulness emphasises *non-judgmental observation* in ever-changing contexts. These observations primarily stem from our *being* mind—the mind that is, quite simply, incapable of doing anything but observing. It doesn't have much room for abstract thought, opinion, strong emotion, internal conflicts. It just IS. It's always there. We can refer to this part of us as "The Curious Observer". The Curious Observer exercises a non-judgemental present moment awareness, and a childlike curiosity of thoughts, senses, emotions, physical sensations, smells, tastes, and external stimulus. The Curious Observer is perpetually relaxed and intrigued, but has no capacity to break things down in a logical or

What Mindfulness Is, and What It Is Not

systematic way, it simply notices with intrigue. Let's not overcomplicate things here—mindfulness is simple!

Luckily for us, we don't have to learn how to become The Curious Observer. In fact, being The Curious Observer may take more *un*learning than learning. This is primarily because The Curious Observer has always been a part of you, from the moment you were born; and will remain with you until the day you die. The Curious Observer does not have any personality traits, no goals or ambitions, no real perspective on anything. It has no judgements, dreams, concerns or worries. The Curious Observer only has one purpose—to experience things just as they are, taking what is offered, without any critical evaluation. It is the part of you that just observes and accepts—because it has no ability to do anything else.

At this juncture, you might be thinking you purchased a book on meditation, which is totally understandable. Meditation and mindfulness are very often lumped into the same category, so I just want to take a moment to address the niggling thought you *may* be having right now—"but isn't meditation the same as mindfulness!?"

Put simply, the answer is a resounding no. While mindfulness and meditation can (and often do) share some similar characteristics, they are not the same thing by any means. Mindfulness is a *quality*, and meditation is a *practice*. It's best to think of meditation in the same vein as something like sports—we all know what a sport is, yet there are hundreds, if not thousands of different sports. We may be excellent at one, and rubbish at another. Meditation is the same. It may be mindful, or transcendental (mantra-orientated), focused, disciplined, or relaxed. Just like sports, there will be some types of meditation you like, and some you don't. Meditation is an amazing activity, and can often be a useful training ground for learning mindfulness, but we don't strictly *need* it to cultivate greater mindfulness in our everyday lives.

Mindfulness, on the other hand, is like being physically fit. Being physically fit will certainly aid our ability to play a lot of different sports effectively, but it will also improve our general health, our mental health, our sleep, our confidence, and our attractiveness among other things. The benefits of being physically fit go far beyond our ability to play sport. We may work to improve a specific type of

What Mindfulness Is, and What It Is Not

fitness for a designated sport, or we may choose to be physically fit for no other reason than we simply *want* to be. Meditation is a practice, and mindfulness is a quality.

So what are the benefits of mindfulness then, you may be asking? If I'm just The Curious Observer, won't that make me an unthinking doofus who just observes things without critical thought with a lazy smile plastered on my face?

Thankfully, there are many benefits to mindfulness–otherwise I probably wouldn't have wasted my time writing this book to share how mindfulness can gradually, incrementally, yet profoundly influence your life in a very positive way. Mindfulness has been scientifically proven (people LOVE to hear scientists support mindfulness) to provide and facilitate the following benefits:

- Relaxation of the mind and the body
- Enhanced cognitive clarity
- Improved intellectual intelligence (and academic success)
- Improved emotional intelligence
- Decreased feelings of stress
- Decreased feelings of unhelpful anxiety
- Decreased severity and symptoms of depression

Maximise Mindfulness, Minimise Mindlessness

- Enhanced emotional regulation and wellbeing
- Greater self-awareness
- Decreased prevalence and effects of strong emotions, such as anger and grief
- Enhanced ability to cope with physical (and mental) illness
- Improved general health, including improved immune response
- Decreased number of sick days, and mental health days, from work
- Decreased need for unhealthy methods of relaxation (drugs, alcohol, junk food, smoking, sexual promiscuity)
- Greater feelings of joy and contentment

These are just some of the benefits, and I would be remiss if I did not mention that some of the benefits you are aiming for may not eventuate (I still get road rage); similarly, some benefits you think you did not need may reveal themselves (I'm incredibly disciplined now—I never used to value discipline *at all!*). Let's just put that down to your body and mind intuitively knowing what you need, and leave it at that. Like The Curious Observer would do.

2

THE MINDLESSNESS PARADOX

We live in an age of mindlessness. We are more stimulated than ever before. We are completely and utterly bombarded with notifications, announcements, updates, crazes, phases, fads and ads. We rarely have time to switch off our busy minds. If we do choose to do nothing, we get FOMO (fear of missing out). We pick our partners off a screen based on their physical attributes. We sit mindlessly in front of the TV gorging on junk food, wondering why we don't have the capacity to be "one of *those* people"—the ones who get up at 5am every day, are in great shape, and run successful businesses. We are constantly comparing and contrasting ourselves, feeling disdain, jealousy, resentment, regret, remorse and perpetual frustration—unaware that we have the internal resources to be content and grateful for what we have, that we are *enough*. We favour the Western ideal of always having to do *something*, unaware that it can be far more helpful to us to do *nothing*. Think to yourself—when was the last time you literally did NOTHING? Just lay down and let whatever happens, happen? For those of you who may think to a previous experience lying down on the grass and looking at the clouds, or sitting in a float tank, or engaging in meditation—did you note how relaxing and calming this was? For those of you who can't remember—do you find it calming and relaxing to be always be *on*?

Put simply, mindlessness is like the bizarro mindfulness. It is a state of cognitive *unawareness* that somewhat ironically comes about as a result of overstimulation. It's like a busy factory where all the machines are working overtime to churn out products, but the products are complete garbage. Almost entirely counterintuitively, our brains in a state of mindlessness are generally buzzing, bouncing and drowning in a soup of complex neurotransmitters and hormones that are intense, and make us act impulsively and in conjunction with strong emotions. But, despite this, we are often so completely overwhelmed that we are in a state of mind that is completely *unaware*. Sound confusing? It is. Allow me to try and demonstrate.

Think to the last time you scrolled through social media for far too long. You may have been scrolling through, watching videos, commenting and liking posts—and yet, you had absolutely no idea how you got there, why you were there, or why you were suddenly feeling emotionally hyper-aroused by the context of the situation. In that trance-like state you were in, however, your brain was going haywire. An intricate combination of neurotransmitters and hormones were firing; your brain was piecing together abstract thoughts, utilising deductive reasoning and emotional processes—yet cognitively, you were perhaps feeling hypnotised, perhaps slovenly, and maybe even unable to move to engage in more productive tasks.

When you're in this state of mind, you might find yourself addicted—unable to extract the slightest amount of willpower needed to wash your clothes, to do the dishes, to tackle an assignment or a work project you desperately need to finish—even to make love!

Yes, we've become masters of utilising dead time, and much of the time it's not even our fault. We wake up early enough to get out the door (most days) to make our way into work either by car, train, bus or bike, before putting in eight to ten hours of our precious time, and then travel back home, barely able to summon the energy to make dinner before passing out in front of the TV, desperate for a drink (or some other vice) that will help our minds to calm down, and yet we keep playing back the entire day, wondering if there was something we could have done different, before pondering larger questions such as "is this really what I want to be doing? Could I be doing something that gives me more life fulfilment?" before returning back to our TVs or the comfort of our smartphones because simply asking these questions (let alone the process of breaking them down analytically), is exhausting. So you continue to avoid these thoughts, perhaps rationalising them or pushing them deep down and still just watching that TV, posting on social media, scrolling, endlessly. It. Is. Exhausting.

In the age of mindlessness, we have effectively become products of our environment. Since the dawn of time, humanity has been sold products—but never before have we *been* the product. We are so stimulated and bombarded by a never-ending, limitless supply of information that promises us a better existence that we're almost totally unaware of the subtle changes in our behaviour which perpetuates the ongoing cycle of advertising-for-consumption. Our immediate environments have become havens for manipulation and exploitation, and we're all privy to it on a practically relentless cycle. Our technology has gotten so unbelievably advanced—so ridiculously quick—that our devices *know* exactly what we want, and provide us with the information necessary to push us down certain paths. For example, if I was to google "COVID-19"—I would be presented with a vast library of articles, videos, photos and social groups that confirm to me the dangers of COVID, including health advice and clinics for vaccination. If my friend, a COVID sceptic, searched for the same thing, he'd have a completely different experience. Much of his information would come from sources who doubt the existence of COVID, or purport that vaccinations are a ploy instigated by the global elite to maximise human control. He would be privy to a virtual library which substantiates his belief.

Yes, we have become perpetual consumers of our immediate short-term environments. Never before has information been so readily accessible at the touch of our fingertips, and never before have we consumed such information at such a rapid and unsustainable pace. We're persistently and voraciously consuming material goods, advertisements, social media, fiction and non-fiction, reality tropes, applications, technological advancements, news articles, fantasy sports (and the list goes on and on and on). Consequently, we have become addicts to our insatiable curiosity and consumption habits. Unfortunately, this leads to us to an inevitable cycle of consuming for short-term pleasure, rather than considering our values or our long-term goals and ambitions.

Part of the issue is that we've become creatures of comfort. Almost everything we purchase, almost every decision we make, is in the pursuit of greater comfort. There's nothing inherently wrong with this—it is part of the human condition after all, to search for greater convenience and comfort. However, it is making us less joyful. Where is the meaning and purpose in one's life if one constantly searches to relieve themselves of all anxiety, struggle, worry and discomfort?

We have forgotten that we only grow through discomfort and suffering.

Consequently, our mindlessness is causing irrevocable damage to our inherent desire to achieve, to be ambitious, to work hard and to remain curious and attentive to attempts to manipulate and exploit. It is absolutely not our fault—but *you* are the best individual available to combat it. It is nobody's fight to undertake but your own. This may be a confronting sentiment, but it is authentic and real and raw. It can be empowering, if you want it to be.

Alas, this brings me to the most important point about mindlessness—it is *not* all doom and gloom. There are some incredible benefits that have come through technological advancements, and I would be remiss if I failed to note that I myself enjoy many of these advancements in the world of comfort, convenience and curiosity. What I am trying to communicate is the need for *balance*. To balance our mindlessness with our mindfulness. To bring a greater sense of purpose, of joy, of contentment, of meaning to our lives. To bridge the gap between our *doing* self and our *being* self.

Is it easy to create balance? No, not always. At times, your journey may seem practically impossible, or at least extremely unenjoyable. I'm reminded of the time I tried to switch my smartphone to a Nokia 3310 to lower my screen time. It was very, very, very difficult—so difficult in fact that I eventually went back to my smartphone. However...

If you're asking the more appropriate question—is it doable? You bet it is! It might take some hard work, some discomfort, some suffering, but as Theodore Roosevelt once said...

"Nothing in this world is worth having or worth doing unless it means effort, pain [and] difficulty"

Keep reading on, and I will delineate just some of the ways you can incorporate more mindfulness into your daily diet, leaving you feeling more confident, relaxed, content, purposeful and joyous in your life—while eliminating some of the mindlessness that frequently leaves you feeling empty, fatigued, and burnt out.

3

HOW TO MAXIMISE MINDFULNESS AND MINIMISE MINDLESSNESS

Now that we have a basic understanding of the principles of mindfulness (present moment awareness) and mindlessness (cognitive unawareness), let's look at some simple, pragmatic and effective ways to reduce the noise and increase the tranquillity.

In order to be as practical as possible, I'm opting to write this out in dot points like a grocery list so you can pick and choose what you desire or need with simplicity and ease.

- **Go into your phone settings and turn off notifications for all your apps.** This will stop you checking your phone every eight seconds, and save you countless minutes, hours, days, and even weeks over the course of the year deleting notifications from apps you didn't even realise you had (or absolutely do not need!)
- **Delete unused apps.** Same as above—why do you need an app you downloaded one year ago that your friend told you to download because it does this thing that you don't need anymore, or never really did need? It's a waste of space, get rid of it!
- **Download a screen time app.** It's a great idea to monitor how many minutes you spend on your phone per day, and track which apps sap the most energy and attention. This will aid your awareness.
- **Turn your phone to greyscale.** There are literally teams of people who are hired to choose specific colours for apps and websites to draw and then hold your attention. Turning your phone to greyscale effectively undoes this process and defeats this marketing ploy in only a matter of seconds. It also makes your phone less appealing, and confuses the hell out of people when they

see your phone is in black and white. That's free entertainment!

- **Watch TV consciously.** Either set some time in advance where you are aware of exactly what you're going to watch, or set a limit—i.e. "I will only watch two episodes of Curb your Enthusiasm before returning to my [insert creative activity here]"
- **Play!** Choosing to move and play over hunching over your screen won't only make you feel better, you'll be a better person for it. Put a song on (I like to use Mariah Carey's 'Emotions' for this) and dance around like a fool. Throw a ball in the air and catch it. Play with a pet, or a child. Whatever it is, don't underestimate the importance of satiating your inner child. We all have one, and they're all desperate to play.
- **Choose NOTHING over SOMETHING!** The next time you feel pressured to do something, lie on your floor and do the exact opposite. It's wild, but incredibly rewarding.
- **Read > Screen.** Kindles don't count here—they're awesome. Choosing to read over choosing your screen activates different parts of the brain responsible for creativity, social interaction,

imagination, comprehension and deductive reasoning. If you are dyslexic or don't enjoy reading—no worries! Get on the audiobooks and get comfy! Reading has a wide variety of benefits (i.e. increased vocabulary) whereas screens (depending on what you do) typically do not. So choose Books over marketing Hooks.

- **Journal.** Journaling is not only an amazing therapeutic tool that helps process difficult thoughts and emotions, it also develops key social skills and helps clarify what is meaningful, purposeful and necessary in your life.
- **Learn a new exercise or sport.** Exercising is awesome, being stronger is always a benefit, being fit is infinitely better than being unfit. You'll be healthier AND more attractive. What have you got to lose?
- **Meditate.** Meditation has been scientifically proven to reduce stress, help manage anxiety, enhance emotional wellbeing and self-awareness, lengthen your attention span, increase empathy and improve sleep (among other things). It can be difficult to get started, but it is incredibly rewarding and a great way to spend time with yourself.

- **Invest in your time.** Basically, go out and spend some money on something you love! You want to take up rollerblading? Go ahead and spend some hard-earned cash on some new rollerblades! This is an investment in your time—you now have a new hobby you can invest your time in when you're feeling mindless or bored.
- **Hold yourself accountable.** This doesn't mean bullying yourself—it means identifying when you've been naughty or unhelpful towards yourself, and making a pledge that you'll do a little better next time. For example, "I told myself I'd only spend two hours on my phone today and go swimming, but I spent four hours on my phone and skipped my swim because I got held up on Instagram. Tomorrow—I'll only spend one hour on my phone and go for an extra-long swim to make up for it!
- **Reflect on your motivations.** This is so important. The next time you do something you love, or something healthy, or something mindful, or something fun—think about WHY! For example, "I chose to play guitar today over watching a film because I desire to be a great guitarist one day" or "I chose to pick up my colouring pad today and

do some colouring because I value creativity and mindfulness."

- This brings me to my next point—**get creative!** Creativity and imagination are an amazing feature of being human and keep us…well, creative…. and human!
- **Discover new interests.** There is an almost infinite number of interests in this world, and each of us have barely begun to scratch the surface of our potential. What does this equation tell us? There is so much that each of us have yet to discover that we will either love, be great at, or will enjoy—so get out there!
- **Think long term > short term.** The easiest way to discern the difference is to ask the question "is this benefiting me today or for the rest of my life?"
- **Reward > Bored.** Think "am I rewarding myself for a job well done, or am I just trying to waste some time mindlessly?" This question works especially well when we engage with mindless activities such as scrolling through social media or watching films—they aren't inherently bad, or things to avoid, but are hardly the best use of our time if we are simply bored.

The aim of these suggestions is ultimately to increase the amount of purpose and meaning in your life by taking you *away* from activities that are generally time-wasting, and directing you *towards* activities that are fulfilling and provide you with a life-affirming vitality—all in the process of helping you become a more well-rounded, interesting and authentic human being.

I'm aware I am giving away some crucial secrets to maximising mindfulness and minimising mindlessness all before Chapter Four. (perhaps I should have waited); but I really wanted you to have some of these practical tips on hand before we move on to other topics that are instrumental in the process of finding more meaning and purpose in your life. So please, keep reading on, and together we'll look at the complex chemical reactions that occur in our body to instances of mindlessness; how to use our emotions, senses, and breath to become more mindful; how to utilise values and gratitude to increase the purposefulness of our lives; how to becoming more accepting; and how to reduce instances of procrastination and distraction.

4

[DOPE]AMINE

Ah dopamine, buzz-word of the 21st century and a sorely misunderstood piece of the human puzzle. Both a neurotransmitter (messengers who send information between neurons and target cells) and a hormone (messengers who help regulate tissues and organs via our blood), dopamine is an important part of our internal circuitry. Outside of its job of maintaining motor control, executive function and arousal, dopamine is that wonderful thing inside us all that motivates, reinforces and rewards. Historically speaking, food, water, sex, exercise, children and our social standing in our tribe were the main instigators of dopamine. As we continue making our way into the 21st century however, dopamine-inducing stimulus has expanded exponentially. We are bombarded with dopamine-inducing materials, and consequently, we have begun to preference short-term pleasure over long-term reward.

On a daily basis, dopamine-inducing stimulus such as smart phones, apps, television, pornography, junk food and drugs have caused us to effectively become dopamine junkies at the expense of our mental health. This is because when we produce dopamine in excess on a continuous basis, it takes our brain a bit of time to adjust and regulate our dopamine in a healthy way. When we bombard our brain with dopamine-inducing stimuli that is neither rewarding nor motivating in the long-term, meaningful and purposeful sense, we are often left feeling anxious, depressed and empty inside.

Addictions are a perfect example of this. As a previous drug addict myself, I think it's befitting to use drug addiction as an example here—but please remember, almost *anything* can turn into an addiction, particularly in the age of increased mindlessness. Let's say someone uses cocaine semi-regularly. At first, it's simply an enjoyable activity which makes them feel more self-confident and talkative in social situations, ultimately giving them feelings of pleasure that they can sustain on a night out (or in). At the biochemistry level, this individual is effectively flooding their brain with dopamine, feeling great when they're in situations where cocaine is being used. They're also forging subconscious associations in the limbic system (the part of the brain associated with memories, emotions, and reinforcing behaviour) that cocaine equals feelings of greater confidence in myself, and more feelings of bliss and joy.

So, what is the consequence of this?

Eventually, the more the individual begins to associate feelings of pleasure with cocaine, the more this is reinforced in the brain at a subconscious level as a necessity to feel pleasure in social situations. The brain is effectively linking social delights with cocaine use—remember, dopamine is the part of our *reward* and *motivation* circuitry.

Let's say the individual now attempts to engage in a social event without the use of cocaine. The brain recognises this by producing decidedly less dopamine, and the individual has...not such a great time. The individual desperately wants to experience this feeling again—because excess dopamine production feels amazing—but the *only* way to achieve this level of pleasure at social events once more is to—you guessed it—take cocaine once again. Thus begins the cycle of addiction. The more prolonged the use, the more the brain has associated cocaine with enjoying social events, so the more the individual has abused cocaine, the less likely it is that they'll be able to enjoy a social event once again without using. In time, this will go beyond social events and the individual will become dependent on using cocaine just to feel a sense of normality.

This is apparent in almost every single illicit drug, but also in addictions to virtually anything else (especially pornography and junk food—sorry to tell you!) Thus, the individual feels an insatiable urge to use their addiction of choice to regain feelings of *normality,* and thus the cycle goes on. To break this cycle, if you've ever had an addiction, is extremely difficult, and generally requires extensive amounts of support.

Humans naturally gravitate towards positive experiences, and we avoid experiences we perceive to be negative. There is absolutely nothing shocking or profound about this. This also occurs in our memories, as we tend to remember fond memories (unless memories are associated with danger), in which we tend to move towards, or similarly avoid situations akin to ones we have experienced before. This is all part of self-preservation and survival, and again, is simply not our fault. We all have addictions, or vices, and it does not mean we are defective or faulty in any way—it generally means we are normal, healthy human beings. If I offered you a bowl of delicious ice cream or steamed broccoli when your blood sugar levels are low, you'd be absolutely justified in choosing the ice cream out of self-preservation.

Fortunately, mindfulness is an effective method to help with a range of addictions, proven to restore grey matter in the brain in just 8 short weeks of regular practice, shrink the part of our brain associated with anxiety, and create more neural connections in the brain associated with learning, memory, and intelligence. Meditation can also be used to facilitate these benefits.

On the next page is a short list of healthy and unhealthy dopamine inducing activities. It is always extremely helpful to identify unhealthy activities that we engage in that produce dopamine, and replace or supplement them with healthy dopamine inducing activities. You might like to simply make a mental list, or, write these down and hold yourself accountable (without being a bully!)

HEALTHY	UNHEALTHY
• Studying/reading • Exercising • Meditation/ Mindfulness • Proper diet • Great sleep • Making love • Playing music • Cuddling a pet or loved one • Sunlight • Creative hobbies	• Social media • Drugs • TV binging • Junk food overindulgence • Pornography • Excessive gaming • Excessive purchasing of material goods • Smoking • High risk, dangerous behaviour

I'm not going to even spend a second pretending I don't engage, or haven't previously engaged in every single activity in the unhealthy dopamine inducing column—most of us have, and that's perfectly okay.

I'm not even going to suggest ceasing activities in the unhealthy column, because many of the activities are not inherently *bad*—they are just activities that typically produce high amounts of dopamine that *can* keep us locked in cycles of addiction and dependence, and *can* keep us *avoiding* all of the wonderful healthy dopamine producing activities in the left column.

What I have learnt is that it's always important to think of things in terms of *moderation* not *cessation* (unless they are truly ruining your life), and so I implore you to begin engaging with more of the healthy activities, and less of the unhealthy, for the sake of your long-term mental health prosperity. The worst thing you can do here is bully yourself for engaging in unhealthy dopamine producing activities. Remember The Curious Observer? It has no time for judgement, only for present moment awareness and curiosity. Now is the time to think about how you might like to change your behaviour to regulate dopamine more effectively; making you happier, healthier, and more fulfilled!

5

THE DO NOTHING APPROACH TO MINDFULNESS

You don't need me to remind you yet again that we live in an increasingly fast-paced and attention-demanding society. Just look around you—it's impossible to ignore!

We are unfortunately taught from a young age to always be doing *something;* that it is never enough to simply sit back and take stock of our thoughts, our body, our emotions, and our surroundings. We learn that to be "successful," we always have to be ON. We understand doing nothing as a crux for the lazy and ambivalent, but luckily for us, we have an almost infinite number of ways to distract us from doing nothing. If we feel bored, we believe we're somehow defective or just not busy enough. If we are invited to a social gathering and we're just not feeling it, we often get FOMO (fear of missing out).

Unfortunately, we are not aided in our journey of doing nothing. The amount of motivational material on platforms like YouTube alone are staggering—in excess of 9 million videos. Most of these are centred on virtually the same topic—how to increase the amount of productive activities in our lives. I'm certainly not suggesting that motivation or discipline are bad things; in fact, you may have noticed that I'm a proponent of consistently learning new strategies to increase our productivity to maximise feelings of meaning and purpose. I'm simply illustrating that if we decide to do nothing in favour of something, we are told we are wasting our time.

Nothing could be further from the truth. In the words of the great Ram Dass:

"The quieter you become, the more you can hear"

Sometimes, doing nothing is infinitely more productive than doing something. Think about

The Do Nothing Approach to Mindfulness

an awkward social interaction you've had recently (we have all had them from time to time). What do you notice about yourself and others when faced with feelings of anxiousness and awkwardness? Likely, you or someone else in the interaction will pull out their phone to distract them from the feelings of discomfort. In the short term, you are now feeling less anxious, finding comfort in your little screen. You are effectively training yourself to *avoid* discomfort, which is understandable—but it is not helpful (that dopamine is now keeping you in a cycle). In the long term, your brain will begin to wire itself to avoid discomfort altogether—and remember, you have an almost infinite number of ways to achieve this. The problem is (and I'm aware I'm repeating myself here) we *always* grow through discomfort. Every crucial lesson you've learned in your life has almost certainly come from discomfort, pain, or suffering. In other words, if you're in an awkward social situation, the best approach is to simply do nothing—notice your feelings, acknowledge them, and keep your phone in your pocket.

There is a mindfulness technique based on this concept that I use daily. I set a timer for a period of time (usually 15-20 minutes is adequate) and I do nothing. There are absolutely no rules. The only rule is that I cannot move until the timer goes off (unless there is an immediate emergency). While it may seem like meditation, it isn't at all. A core component of meditation is to usually focus on something (like the breath for instance). This activity is actively *non*-focusing.

While it sounds bizarre, this exercise is one of the best available for you to achieve those "AHA" moments. The moments when things come together; the realisations, epiphanies and observations about yourself that are crucial in your quest to become a better and more fulfilled person. So try it out—the next time you have some free time and feel you must be doing *something*, choose instead to lie or sit down, and do *nothing*. You might be amazed at what you discover about yourself.

6
GETTING EMOTIONAL

Did you know that we make the majority of our decisions in life based on our emotions? Yes, even those who appear to be robotic in their logic and rationalising are in the same boat. So what really are emotions? Although there is no universally agreed definition, I will employ the term "action-requiring neurological impulses," once taught to me by my incredible meditation coach Matt Young. Before we continue, it is important to acknowledge that emotions are often culturally defined, meaning that the expression, or even feeling of particular emotions may be encouraged in one culture, and completely shirked in another (men crying or expressive grief, for example). Awareness of this fact will help facilitate the processing of emotions in a technique I've outlined at the end of this chapter.

Now let's break this down—an emotion, although (very) often perceived as seemingly unhelpful or irrational, is an action-requiring neurological impulse. "Action-requiring," in terms of the human psyche, implies...that an action, or behaviour, or choice must be made in the pursuit of—you guessed it—self-preservation. So already we've established that emotions are something that require *immediate action* by the individual for the sake of self-preservation. Then, emotions are "neurological impulses"—so effectively, we have zero control over when, or if, or how an emotion occurs. So put that all together and we have something that spurs to life within us impulsively, and that requires attention and likely a subsequent action or behaviour for the sake of self-preservation.

In other words, emotions demand to be listened to. More importantly, they *deserve* to be listened to, because they occur impulsively for the sake of our own benefit, even if sometimes they are a little misguided. Emotions are imperfect, just like us, but their intentions are always good.

Even though our emotions are just trying to help us out, how seldom do we spend time listening to them? We so often preference logic or rationalising to the incredibly worthwhile endeavour of spending time experiencing our emotions, because they can often seem unhelpful, painful, or just cruel and unreasonable. I mean, who wants to sit with the feelings of grief or fury!?

It is so, so, so important to point out here that emotions are NEUTRAL. There is no such thing as a "good" or "bad" emotion. Sure, some emotions feel awful (fear, anger, depression) and some feel great (joy, love, happiness) but ultimately, they are all still completely and utterly neutral. While happiness is considered to be a positive emotion, think—would it be appropriate to feel happy when seeing someone sleeping on the street mid-winter? Would it be okay to feel elated and joyful after learning that someone you are close to has passed away? The answer is no.

By the same token, would it not be extremely helpful to be feeling fear while walking through a dark forest at night? Would it not be extremely useful to feel a white hot rage when you're life is being threatened by another person, or to feel grief and depression when you've lost someone very close to you?

Emotions are great at revealing themselves in context, because they are part of our self-preservation. Unfortunately, they are sorely misunderstood, they suffer from a lack of empirical studies and wider exploration, and they are, on our part, often ignored or come second in preferential treatment to logic, cognitive deconstruction or rationalisation.

There is a wonderful adage that is simple and beautiful in regards to emotions—"we have to feel to heal." Launching from this beautifully simplistic but ultimately profound quote, I'd like to suggest that emotions deserve our time and attention, our gratitude and our respect in order to aid our healing and personal growth. Whenever I feel a strong emotion, I spend some time with it and allow it to naturally process itself. The average emotion lasts about 90 seconds, so this process is not overwhelmingly difficult or time-consuming, but it is extremely helpful.

So how do we process an emotion? Luckily for us, an emotion is *always* associated with a felt sense—

meaning you can literally *feel* any given emotion in the body if you give it your attention.

I am going to employ an emotion processing technique that is a variation of Tara Brach's RAIN method to guide you through a very simple, yet very effective method to experience and process emotions in a non-confrontational and gentle way. For reference, RAIN stands for Recognise, Allow, Investigate and Nurture. My homage to this famous and very efficacious technique is FEEL—Focus, Engage, Expand and Love.

THE FEEL EXERCISE

First, find where the emotion is located in your body, and to the best of your ability, keep your *focus* on that sensation. Identify what emotion you might be feeling. This may be done in reverse, if you know the emotion already (i.e. "I'm angry and can feel a pressure in my head"). The sensation may be completely pervasive, or it may be localised in one area. Just take some time to find it, and keep your focus on the most pressing area that is requiring your attention. For example, you might find that a heaviness in your chest is the most demanding sensation and recognise this as sadness, or you may already know the emotion as, let's say, anxiety, and notice a swirling sensation in your stomach. Focusing on this sensation is effectively giving your attention to your emotion. You are acknowledging that your emotion deserves and often requires your full attention to be properly processed.

You might like to think in terms of a scientist who has just made a brand-new discovery, or a child exploring a new and exciting environment. Think about the kind of questions they would ask. You might like to question what the emotion looks like, does it have a shape, or texture? Does it have a colour? Does it present itself as an image? Is it big, or small? Does it perhaps have a scent, or even a taste to it?

The next step is to *engage*. Once you have found and focused on the emotion, you are now engaging with it—like you would a child who is distressed. Just like you'd approach a distressed child, it is very helpful to greet the emotion in a non-threatening and soothing way. In the first step, which is to focus, you are observing the emotion and bringing to your attention, kind of like watching something from afar. In this step, you are moving towards that emotion, acknowledging that you can see, hear, and feel this emotion, that you are giving it your full attention, respect, and consideration.

You may notice through your engagement that you are literally giving up on the idea that you can force or will your emotions to do what you want. Instead, you are simply acknowledging the emotion as it is and moving *toward it,* rather than running *away* from it. Remember: it is counterproductive to fight emotions, or push them away, because they are part of your self-preservation process. So do the opposite. Engage with them. The emotion might be very painful, or cause you extreme discomfort, but over time, you will notice that this emotion cannot hurt you, and allowing it to be in its own space with full respect is far more helpful than trying to push it away, or shove it down.

Step three is to *expand.* Once you have focused on the emotion, and engaged with it, you'll want to give it space to operate. It already has *some* space to exist (or else you wouldn't be able to find it) but likely, it is confined or constrained because our natural inclination with emotions is to try and limit their ability to control our behaviour. So once again, we're going to try and do the opposite and actually give the emotion space by *expanding* the area in which it currently occupies. This is most effectively done by noticing our breath, and breathing in to the space in which the emotion lies. This can be very difficult to do initially, so don't despair and just keep at it! While you're breathing into the space around the emotion, you will likely begin to notice that it feels a little bit freer, a little bit less cramped. Keep up with this process as long as you need, until the emotion has enough space to breathe itself.

It is very important to note that this step is often enough to effectively process the emotion. You might take a deep breath, or find that your focus on the emotion has dissipated significantly. That is perfectly normal. If this happens for you, and you're worried because there is a final step to complete (love) don't stress! It means you have successfully processed an emotion and you should be very proud of that. Similarly, if you're feeling like you have *not* found any significant changes with the emotion, or that perhaps it has even become stronger, that is also perfectly normal. Just remind yourself that this emotion exists only to serve your self-preservation in the only way it knows how, that it cannot physically hurt you, and continue with the process of giving it space. If this fails, you can run through the entire process again. I have to do this *all the time* with especially stubborn or uncomfortable emotions, so please—*don't bully yourself!*

The final step is to *love*. This is the simplest step in the process. All that needs to be done here is to recognise that you're not defined by one emotion, and *thank* your emotion for revealing itself. Even more, you can thank yourself for undergoing this process. This is the self-love, or self-respect part of the process—recognising that emotions reveal themselves indiscriminately and impulsively on a whim because they're trying to be helpful. Therefore, emotions deserve our love. So do that. Give thanks to your emotion, to yourself. Be proud of yourself. Blow a kiss to your emotion if you like—whatever you need to do to convey that you love your emotion for being there for you, that you love yourself for trying to be a better person.

Please attempt this process the next time you are feeling overwhelmed by a particular emotion. While you may not feel better after (feeling better is sometimes a helpful by-product of this exercise, but it is not the intention), you will hopefully process an emotion that you would otherwise have ignored or pushed down—and that, in itself, is a beautiful thing that will make you grow a little as a human being.

Remember to FEEL to HEAL.

7

SENSING OUR SENSES

One of the first techniques I learned as a young and willing practitioner of meditation was how to preference my senses to facilitate calmness and tranquillity. In fact, one of the biggest roadblocks to my daily meditation practice had been distractions—often of the auditory kind. I'd get settled, I'd begin to notice my thoughts coming and going, my breath, and then I'd hear roadworks going on outside and become furious! I spoke to my teacher about this, and what he suggested changed everything. He actually suggested *focusing* on my distraction!

"If something is annoying you or distracting you, focus only on that," he said.

I did, and low and behold, I wasn't furious anymore. I became more settled, and was able to continue meditating without "distraction" because the distraction became my focus. By focusing on my distraction, I took the power away from it and simply accepted it as an unavoidable part of life. Meditating on breath and there's a possum outside screeching and banging on my roof? No worries. That becomes my focus. Focusing on my body and suddenly noticing an insatiable urge to itch? That becomes my focus. Meditating on emotions and noticing my dog has farted right next to me and it absolutely stinks!? That becomes my focus (albeit, not my favourite thing to focus on!)

What I ultimately realised is that my teacher had surreptitiously asked me to preference my senses while meditating to help facilitate feelings of calm. I also learned that focusing on the senses is absolutely *not* something that has to happen during meditation—it can be done anywhere, anytime, any part of the day; and it is almost *always* calming and peaceful.

It wasn't until later that I began to learn *why*

senses facilitated feelings of calm and presence, but once I did, I was able to apply this consistently. In essence, I acknowledged that the senses are closely aligned with our being mind; the relaxed, calm and composed counterpart to our doing mind. Remember The Curious Observer? That's them!

When we are engaged with our doing mind (which we are a majority of the time) we are generally in a state of perpetual preoccupation with thought and cognitive analysis. Our doing mind has little chance for rest, and certainly has little interest in our being mind taking the reins. Our doing mind is like a bustling city in peak hour, made up of a nearly endless multitude of different people, businesses, transportation, languages and cultures. It is constantly analysing, assessing, and making connections.

Subsequently, our doing mind tends to be:

- Contemplative, analytical, process-based, informed by opinions, judgements and perspectives
- Restless
- Filled with worries, plans, concerns, what-ifs, fantasies and inner dialogues

- Engrossed with cycling relentlessly through past mistakes and future concerns without resolution
- Lacking in awareness for what is happening in the present

Contrarily, our being mind is like a serene and quaint country town on a Sunday morning. There is little movement, it is slow paced and quiet, the air is fresh and the stressors minimal.

Our being mind tends to be:

- Focused on the present moment
- Observant, non-judgemental and curious
- Preoccupied with immediate tasks
- Less likely to be concerned with 'attacking' thoughts
- Less likely to be overwhelmed by strong emotions
- Able to accept and process difficult thoughts with a greater capacity

This is not to say our being mind is superior to our doing mind; quite the contrary. This is just to illustrate that in a world increasingly filled with extreme preoccupations, demanding stimuli, attention-stealing advertising, and dopamine-sapping technological devices, a simple, yet highly effective method to calm our internal circuitry and find peaceful equilibrium is simply to focus on our senses.

When we are engaged with our doing mind, we are typically engaged with our Beta Brainwaves. These brainwaves, when illustrated on paper, typically resemble a rollercoaster—there are steep inclines and declines. The peaks and troughs are jagged and sharp.

When we are engaged with our being mind, we are typically engaging with our Alpha Brainwaves. These brainwaves are more accurately represented as gentle waves on an ocean—the inclines and declines are much smoother. The waves are gradual and mild.

What this demonstrates is that we are typically calmer and more relaxed when we are engaged in activities that promote Alpha Brainwaves. Alpha Brainwaves are typically utilised when we are sleeping, meditating, having a nice warm bath, listening to gentle music, cuddling, relaxing, and going for a gentle stroll in nature. Of course, we can't do these things all the time, especially when we're at work, doing life admin tasks (cleaning, organising, shopping etc.) or just generally being a human being with a normal array of stressful and demanding things on our plate.

However, by sensing our senses, we can effectively engage with these Alpha Brainwaves and incorporate more of our being mind into everyday circumstances. This will facilitate feelings of relaxation and calm, especially in events where it may be wholly necessary. Sensing our senses is actually extremely easy and intuitive—it requires no teaching because you already know how to do it. The most important thing is to *remember* to do it, and this is often the most difficult part of sensing.

Something as simple as eating a meal can be an overwhelmingly powerful and wonderful experience, if only we remember how to remain engaged with our senses. Below is a very simple technique that demonstrates how simple it is to engage with all five senses while eating something delicious.

SENSORY FOOD EXERCISE

Go ahead now and find something small and yummy. It can be a grape, a piece of chocolate, some cheese—whatever you enjoy. The first step in this exercise is to turn off any external distractions (TV, phone, music etc.) so you can fully experience your food in the moment.

First, observe the food visually, engaging with the sense of *Sight*. What colours are present? Is it large, or small? Round, cubed, or jagged? Does it have contrasting elements, such as competing colours, or textures? Is there anything else noticeable about this food?

Now, we're going to engage with the sense of *Smell*. Go ahead and bring the food up to your nostrils and take a big whiff. Allow the scent to permeate your nostrils, perhaps taking into account the simplicity or the complexity of your foods' scent. Is it clean, and fresh? Perhaps it is stinky, or poignant. It may have a variety of different scents—try to identify what they are.

Next, place the piece of food in your mouth—but do not chew just yet! We are going to engage with the sense of *Touch*. Simply roll the piece of food around your mouth, allowing your tongue to slide over it, feeling it against the roof of your mouth, against your teeth. Just spend a few moments doing this, working out the different textures of your piece of food, noticing how it feels to have it in your mouth, tantalising your senses.

Now you can begin chewing your chosen piece of food. You are now engaging with the sense of *Taste*. Notice the different flavours erupting as you chew on your food. Observe the peaks and troughs of the flavours, acknowledging the rise and falls of taste intensity, or perhaps even different flavours coming to the forefront of your attention.

As you are chewing, close your eyes and listen to the sounds your jaw is making as you chew up and down, side to side. Notice how loud it can be to listen to yourself eat with no other distractions—the sound of chewing, of salivating, of swallowing.

That's it! This is very simple exercise you can do whenever you're eating or drinking something that nourishes you. Of course, not all of us are interested in engaging with our senses when we eat—it might be the only time of day where we can watch TV, or communicate with our family, or we may just not be that interested by our food. That is perfectly okay, remember—that is only an example of how mindfulness can be applied to eating, when we are so often distracted from this very simple task by an array of mindlessness-inducing activities. You might prefer to engage with your senses while going for a walk, or engage with your senses while playing a musical instrument, or cuddling a pet, or swimming in the ocean, or having a shower—there is no right or wrong.

To help facilitate this process further, I will provide a very simple mindfulness technique that can be utilised whenever you have a spare five to ten minutes in your day. This will help ground you wherever you are, and help to enable feelings of calm, relaxation, and present moment awareness.

THE FIVE SENSES EXERCISE

1. Notice five things you can see, wherever you are, in your immediate environment
2. Close your eyes, and notice four things you can physically feel within your body, or around you. This might be a gentle wind, or, a feeling of discomfort within the body. It may be your breath, or your hands on your lap, or your butt on a chair
3. Notice three things you can hear. They might be far away, or close, loud or soft, annoying or calming
4. Notice two things you can taste. Maybe you've had just a meal and a drink and you can taste the residual flavours on your tongue—maybe you're

imaginative, and you're simply thinking of things you'd like to taste at this moment
5. Take a deep breath in through the nose. What do you smell? Identify just one scent, and observe.

8

REMEMBERING TO BREATHE

Believe me, I *know* how frustrating it is to be told to breathe. We breathe all the time subconsciously, so why do people tell me to be aware of it!? Why don't they mind their own breathing!?

It took me a while to realise, until someone so poignantly pointed out to me, that breathing *always* occurs in the present moment. Once a breath is breathed, it cannot be breathed again. We also cannot will ourselves to breathe a future breath—because it plainly does not exist yet. Every breath we take is not only unique, it occurs right here and now, never to exist again.

From the moment we're born, until the day we die, we are always breathing in and out. We take around 20,000 breaths every day, which equals 140,000 in a week—that's about 8 million breaths in a year. If you're lucky enough to live until you're 80, you'll have breathed approximately 670 million times. Every single one of these breaths are pivotal in keeping you alive—yet how many of these breaths will you have even been aware of?

The reason why it is so effective to focus on the breath as a calming mechanism is that it is the perfect way to ground us. In any moment, we will be breathing, it always occurs in the present, it reminds us that we are alive, it feels really good, and the act of focusing on something as simple as breathing can often take us out of our own doing mind and help us engage solely with the being mind.

It is no mistake that meditation practitioners, athletes, military personnel, anger management participants, therapists, shamans (and the list goes on) focus on the breath as a way of grounding, relaxing, or improving the cardiovascular system or immune system. The breath is simply awesome—it only gives to us, and it never takes. What a perfect mechanism to be grateful for, and show a little love and attention to.

Rather than dedicate an entire chapter to how awesome the breath is, let's get extremely practical and focus on a few breathing techniques that are often utilised for specific purposes. That way, you'll have multiple breathing techniques at your disposal to employ when needed. How great is that!?

The following breathing techniques can be repeated as many times as you like, or feel comfortable doing. None of them are dangerous. They may make you feel pretty good, perhaps a bit lightheaded—but this is perfectly normal, so just go with it. You can engage with any of these breathing technique at any time, at any place—so long as you're not too loud with your breaths. I will also identify what circumstances these breathing methods are best used in.

BOX BREATHING (4X4X4X4)

Box Breathing is famously used by US Navy Seals when they're plunged into the icy depths of the Pacific with their hands tied behind their back, genuinely struggling for life itself. It is very simple to learn, remember, and execute. After a few minutes, you should be feeling more present, more focused, and just...better. This breathing technique is most helpful when you're feeling **overwhelmed, stressed or anxious.**

Start simply by breathing in for a count of four seconds, through the nose. You might try to breathe in and fill your lungs to the max if it is comfortable.

Hold this breath for four seconds.

Breathe out through the mouth for a count of...you guessed it, four seconds. If you have had breathed a full breath, make sure to exhale to the same degree, emptying your lungs of the precious breath you inhaled just eight seconds ago.

Now hold your empty lungs for a count of four seconds.

That's it! It's a simple trick that will only take a few seconds to learn, and you can apply it anywhere as a pick-me-up or as a simple strategy to employ when you're feeling overwhelmed. I'll give you a moment to do this in your own time.

THE 4, 7 & 8

The 4, 7 & 8 is a similar, yet slightly different method to Box Breathing that was first developed by Dr.

Andrew Weil, and based on an ancient synchronistic yogic breathing technique known as pranayama. The 4, 7 & 8 was designed for deep relaxation, and has emerged as a popular and highly effective method to facilitate and instigate sleepiness. This breathing method is best used for **sleep and/or deep relaxation.**

This technique requires more practice than the Box Breathing technique, but the effects are profound. You might need to read through this technique and break it down incrementally before giving it a shot, but I will do my best to communicate the best method so you can nail it every time.

Start by breathing in through the nose for a count of four seconds. Try to fill those lungs—you want your belly to expand outward, as you breathe deeply in to your diaphragm.

Hold this breath for a count of seven seconds.

Breathe out for a count of eight seconds. This can be difficult to adjust to. A handy tip is to purse your lips, and keep your breath as steady as possible, like a reverse whistle, or like you're gently blowing up a balloon, as you exhale.

Breathe in again through the nose (for four seconds) immediately after breathing out, and continue this process for as long as possible. The perfect harmonies of each process form a symphony of relaxation and focus, keeping you invested in the goal of relaxation.

LION BREATH

The Lion Breath method can be quite loud, visibly noticeable and very humorous for yourself or anyone else witnessing it, so it is not as inconspicuous as the other breathing techniques—thus it is best used in your own personal space (I like to use this in my car). This technique is best used as an **energy boost** or to reduce the physiological effects of **strong emotions**.

Start by breathing in through your nose for however long feels comfortable. Like the other breathing techniques, try your best to feel your belly expand, taking in as much air as you can.

Now, stick your tongue out as far as it will go, trying your best to lick your chin.

Breathe out through your mouth, and let out a loud and aggressive "EGHHHHHH" sound with your tongue still pointed out and down. Really try to make this as loud as possible, releasing the air quickly and efficiently.

Remembering to Breathe

Repeat this process until you start giggling uncontrollably, or until you feel more energised, or less physically effected by a strong emotion.

I hope you've tried and enjoyed at least one of these breathing techniques while reading this chapter, but if not, I truly hope you've bookmarked this part of the book to remind yourself that there are options to calming yourself when you're feeling overwhelmed. Often, it is as simple as remembering to breathe.

9

GRATITUDE & THE SHOULDA, WOULDA, COULDAS

"She is a wise woman who does not grieve for the things she has not, but rejoices for those which she has"

—Epictetus

Gratitude is the key to joy, contentment, peace and happiness in one's own life. We simply cannot experience true fulfilment without a sense of gratitude, because without it, we are simply preoccupied with the concepts more, bigger, or better. Much of the time, *comparison* is the source of all other feelings that stem from ingratitude—jealousy, envy, frustration, dissatisfaction, low self-esteem, anger, contempt and resentment. The beauty of gratitude is that it is inherently mindful. It takes us away from frames of mind buoyed by mindlessness, such as futile comparison, and brings us into the present moment—aiding a sense of positive presence.

This brings to my first point about gratitude:

We can't experience joy without gratitude

Yes, without the ability to give thanks for what we have, how can we ever enjoy what we *do* have? If I were to say, buy a new car, and my response was "I wish I had more money to buy a better car," would I ever enjoy driving my new car around town, taking friends to social engagements, driving out to the country with my dog to go on a hike, or going to the drive in to watch a new film? The answer is likely no. I'd probably be consumed by feelings of ingratitude stemming from unhealthy feelings of comparison—"I really wanted *that* car! Damn that person for making more money than me! My car is a piece of junk!"

Before I continue to unpack the complex framework of gratitude, my conscience dictates that

Maximise Mindfulness, Minimise Mindlessness

I *must* clarify something. Every single person is born with a desire to want more than what they currently have. It is a complex part of our survival circuitry, which our anxiety will tell us was incredibly useful some 100,000 years ago, but is a little outdated now. We will ALL, at times, feel envious, jealous, or full of desire for things we currently don't have. It is perfectly healthy and perfectly normal to compare ourselves to others and despair what we would like but do not currently have. However, it is generally not *helpful*. But please don't beat yourself up about this the next time you're feeling ungrateful. In the words of the late great Robin Williams uttered in ground-breaking film *Good Will Hunting*—"it's not your fault."

This brings me to my second point about gratitude:

> Every person compares, and every person feels ungrateful, sometimes

Luckily for us, being grateful is actually extremely easy and intuitive. It can be taught, learned, experienced or instinctual; yet we rarely reflect on it. We often preference our "shoulda woulda coulda's" instead ("I shoulda got that promotion!" "I woulda been the best pick for captain of the football team!" "I coulda done that way better!"). As I mentioned, this is all perfectly normal, yet often not very helpful. We've all been guilty of utilising the "shoulda woulda coulda's"—me included—and I imagine I'll be guilty of this countless more times before my final breath!

The simple fact is, "shoulda woulda coulda's" are generally a futile and retrospective attempt to gain control over a situation we probably didn't have any control over in the first place. It is much healthier to simply recognise this, and then name something we're grateful for in that moment. This brings me to my third point about gratitude:

We all have SOMETHING to be grateful for!

Even at rock bottom, when the walls of our life feel like they are crumbling in on us, when we have nothing left to give, no support, no ability to perceive a future, there is ALWAYS something to be grateful for. Thankfully, many of us will never know what it is like to experience such a dark time; yet even in that moment, there is room for gratitude. This person is still breathing. They are experiencing a very real array of human emotions (as devastating as they may be). There is little room for things to get worse. They might even have somebody in their life (a loved one, a pet). They likely are still able to feed and hydrate themselves. They likely have a roof over their heads and a place to sleep. They likely have beautiful memories of a time that was much better to reflect on. They may still have their health. Again, it is not for me to engage in supposition about what this hypothetical person is going through, I am simply illustrating that even to someone who is at the lowest point, there are still things to grateful for. Often, all it takes is moving away from the "shoulda woulda coulda's" and asking the question "what do I have to be thankful for right now?" to facilitate feelings of gratitude.

I'd like you to undertake a very simple exercise in gratitude right now. This is something that shouldn't take more than a few minutes, is easy to remember, and can be completed virtually any time of the day, whether you have access to a phone, a pen and paper, or simply your own mind.

The exercise is to simply write five things you are grateful for. To make things a little bit more comprehensive and to widen your perspective a tad, you're going to write these five things in accordance with the prompts below. Give it a shot, and note how you feel!

GETTING GRATEFUL EXERCISE

1. Name something incredibly small that you're grateful for today (i.e. I'm grateful for the yummy cup of coffee I had this morning)
2. Name something you're grateful for this week (i.e. I'm grateful for the party I attended on Saturday)
3. Name a personality trait, or a value of yours, that you're grateful for (i.e. I'm grateful for my sense of humour)
4. Name a person, or animal, you are grateful to have in your life (i.e. I'm grateful for my dog, Charlie)

Name something large you are grateful for (I'm grateful for the fact I live in Australia)

See how easy it is to be grateful! The best part is, once you start practising gratitude regularly, you'll get really good at being grateful in the moment. Subsequently, your internal circuitry and outlook will begin to change, and you'll notice a substantial shift in your daily contentment, joy, meaning and purpose. For example, you might go to your favourite ice-cream parlour and notice your favourite flavour is sold out. Rather than say "the pistachio gelato shouldn't have sold out already!" you might actually think "I'm so grateful they're open! I love ice-cream!"

That's a bad example for a profound idea, but hey—I'm grateful for being a total dag—and I'm grateful for you reading that.

10

MEDITATION: MYTHS AND MISCONCEPTIONS

The purpose of this chapter is simply to dispel some common meditation myths and misconceptions. Because this book is predominately about mindfulness, I don't want to conflate the practice of meditation with the *quality* that is mindfulness. Remember: while meditation and mindfulness can and often share similar characteristics, they are different, and they are not mutually exclusive. You can think of mindfulness as being like a river and meditation as a boat. They do not need each other (you can take a boat on any body of water) but often they work harmoniously together to get you where you need to go.

Furthermore, I also feel that I'll be doing you—and the practice of meditation itself—a grave disservice trying to cover the extensive and historical practice in this chapter alone. Meditation deserves its own library of books—not simply a short chapter in a book on mindfulness and mindlessness. My hope is that, through dispelling some of the common myths and misconceptions about meditation, you'll be inspired to start a meditation practice in your time, exploring the vast world of meditation styles and approaches in an attempt to find one (or several) that you gel with.

One of the common misconceptions about meditation is that you have to *stop* thinking. Contrary to this opinion, the most effective way to calm your mind is not by attempting to stop thoughts, but rather allowing your thoughts to come and go whilst remaining as The Curious Observer. The effort to empty your mind will virtually guarantee that you feel agitated, discouraged and stressed.

Go ahead and try it now—force yourself to stop thinking entirely and just notice what happens…

...Did you notice the futility in that exercise? That's because the mind is *designed* to think, in the same way our eyes are designed to see, and our ears designed to hear. Any attempt to stop the process of the mind doing what it is intended to do will only leave you feeling irritated, and will probably lead to some severe self-bullying.

Another common misconception about meditation is the idea of the "Magic Pill"—that if you begin meditation, all of your worries, concerns, problems, frustrations, irritations, self-esteem issues and ambivalences will be magically fixed because meditation is a healer of all. I'm not saying it *can't* be, but it is highly impractical and logistically improbable. Meditation itself cannot heal the deep recesses of your heart and soul. It can, however, be utilised alongside other holistic practices to make you a happier, healthier and more fulfilled human being. I adopted meditation and mindfulness into my daily life during my drug rehabilitation stage, but it also took years of psychotherapy, intensive exercise, a complete overhaul of my sleep and diet regimes, a support network, and further meaning and purpose orientated activities to help bring me to where I am today. If someone tells you meditation can "fix" everything, take it with a big grain of salt.

It is commonplace in meditation practice to begin getting sleepy, possibly even falling asleep during this time. This is because an extended meditation session will activate those Alpha brainwaves we spoke of before, and take you often into a trance-like, hypnotic state. If you feel sleepy here, that's pretty normal considering what is going on inside your brain. They call it falling asleep for a reason—we have no control over it! If you begin meditation and notice you keep teetering on the edge of consciousness, or falling asleep—that's perfectly okay and completely understandable! It doesn't mean you've failed; on the contrary, you can consider it a success because you brought yourself into such a relaxed state that your body took the hint and drifted off to sleep. Well done I say!

Below are some other common meditation myths and misconceptions:

- **I must remain perfectly still with my eyes closed.** Nope. You can meditate in any position that is comfortable for you and adjust and scratch as you need. Ever heard of walking meditation? That can be incredibly difficult when your eyes are closed! You may keep your eyes open, or choose to close

them. Most people prefer to close them, but hey—meditation is unique, just like you. Do what makes you comfortable
- **I have to commit to one style of meditation and stick with it religiously.** Nonsense. How can one find the most appropriate form of meditation without some exploration? Me personally, I use a variety of different meditation styles depending on what I need from my sessions (energy, relaxation, focus, discipline, emotional processes etc.)
- **I must sit in traditional lotus position.** Have you ever tried to sit in the traditional lotus position? It sucks. It's really uncomfortable for a lot of people, and this position is generally favoured by the naturally flexible and/or consistent yoga practitioners. There is absolutely nothing wrong with it, if its comfortable for you, but by the same token, it is also absolutely not necessary
- **Meditation is too hard.** It can be, but it doesn't have to be. Find a style and a time that works for you, explore, and get comfortable. Become The Curious Observer and work with your distractions, and don't beat yourself up. You'll find it is not as daunting and scary as you think

- **My mind must not wander or I've failed.** Minds are going to wander all the time during meditation. Eventually, it may wander less—but don't stress out about this. You might like to simply acknowledge when this happens and bring your attention back to whatever it is you were focusing on (breath, emotions, body, mantra etc.)
- **If I get distracted, I'm doing it wrong.** If you get distracted, you're a human being. Work with your distractions and make them the focus of your meditation on the fly. It's fun, and effective!
- **I'm just too busy to incorporate meditation into my life.** You can meditate in 30 seconds or 20 minutes. You can meditate on a bus, at traffic lights, on a walk or while having a shower. You're not too busy—you just don't want to. That's okay too—but don't use the "too busy" spiel
- **Meditation just isn't for me.** It may not be for you, and that's okay—although, I can almost guarantee that the vast majority of those who have uttered this sentiment have tried one or few meditation variants, had a poor teacher, listened to awful guided meditations online, or have not read this book chapter! If you want to incorporate meditation into your life, I *promise* you'll find

one you like, if you stick with it long enough. Remember—I stormed out of my first meditation session and yelled about what "total bullshit" it was. Now I teach it. Go figure!

According to the wonderful Jason Siff, meditation teacher extraordinaire who spent 30 years trying to answer the question of what meditation is, meditation is simply whatever happens during your experience, during the process of meditating. In other words, if you sit, lie, stand, walk or float with the intention to meditate, no matter what happens during your experience—you have successfully meditated.

Sounds too simple to be true right?

What I love about this idea is that it is beautiful and profound in its simplicity, and an incredibly influential way to help people learn the skill of meditation without putting any pressure or judgement on them. For others, this might seem a bit abstract, or airy-fairy—and that's fine too. Meditation certainly comes in all different shapes and sizes, time lengths and environments, but what seems be a consistent theme in meditation are the ideas of focus, acknowledgement, and present moment awareness. Just like with mindfulness,

The Curious Observer may emerge to explore its environment like a playful child or intrigued scientist to notice what's going on—free of the constraints of critical analysis and judgement (the scientist would likely do that after exploring the environment, in a lab…and the child would likely berate their caregivers with a long stream of "why" questions!).

While I have mentioned (and stand by) the assertion that meditation cannot be covered in this chapter, it is my intention to dispel the myths of meditation to make meditation more approachable for you. In order to do that, I've broken down in the most simplistic way what meditation basically looks like in a very rudimentary four step process:

1. Focus on something
2. Lose focus as your mind wanders
3. Recognise you've lost focus and bring your attention back
4. Repeat

There is a lot to unpack within this four-step process, most of which is entirely unique to each person, but the idea is very sound. You can try this process now simply by using the breath.

UNCOMPLICATED BREATH MEDITATION

1. Focus on your breath as it moves endlessly in and out. You might like to focus on the breath as it enters your nostrils, or feel your belly expanding or contracting, or take a more universal view of the process of your breathing
2. Inevitably, you'll notice that your mind has a mind of its own, and you've completely lost your focus on the breath. Acknowledge this, and…
3. Bring your attention back to the breath
4. This process will inevitably repeat over and over and over again until your finish your meditation

It's really that simple, although as I've mentioned—there a countless number of different meditation variants you can try. I truly hope this chapter on meditation has made you feel a little bit more confident in pursuing it as a regular practice. It's entirely possible for you to take up a regular meditation practice today, armed with only a simple intention to meditate to receive benefits. Meditation will absolutely aid your journey of mindfulness, while giving you the self-awareness you might need to excise mindlessness from your life. Meditation is awesome.

11

VAL-U-ES

Values are our internal moral compass. If we were on a boat looking for our own personal island paradise in which to retire fat and jolly, values would be our map, rudder and oars.

Values convey to us, in no uncertain terms, what we stand for, what we care deeply about, and what we want our lives to be remembered for. Values motivate, inspire and guide us towards greener pastures, and each step we take in alignment with our values just feels worthwhile and resolute. Conversely, when we act in rejection of our values, we often feel empty, lost, and inauthentic. We float aimlessly in our boats with no map for direction, no rudder for stability, and no oars for propulsion.

Unfortunately, you could throw a stone and hit someone who couldn't tell you what their core values are off the top of their head. Values may be inherently unique and meaningful to everyone—yet hardly anyone spends time reflecting on what these values actually are, and even less time considering how their values drive their behaviour! For an important piece of the human puzzle, values are less regarded in our modern society than personality traits, career choices, and economic stability. Ironically, without a firm understanding of one's values, an individual will deduce little enjoyment from their job or cash flow, and will often feel totally insecure and unimpressed with their personality.

Values are cross-contextual, fluid and transcendental. They are cross-contextual because our values can effectuate our behaviour in almost every single circumstance. One of my core values, for example, is empathy. I can be empathic with a family member in crisis, and I can be empathic towards someone I see sleeping rough. I can be empathic in my place of work (in fact, I must be) and empathic to my dog, Charlie, when he hurts his leg on a run.

Values are fluid, because as humans, we change throughout our life cycle. Our goals, ambitions and desires are constantly changing as we age, just as traumatic events may irrevocably alter our personalities or outlook, and extreme successes may adjust our life paths. Empathy may not be one our core values as a young person navigating the job market and trying to accumulate wealth, for example, but may become our penultimate value when we have a child. Conversely, we may be an extremely hardworking lawyer who values industry, productivity and ambition, until one day we decide we dislike our job, and we quit to go live in remote Alaska, living off the land with no need for material possessions outside of what is necessary—thereby our values might alter drastically to include things like independence, tranquillity and sustainability. This last example isn't *likely* to happen, but I've been watching an amazing show recently about people living in Alaska and I just had to incorporate an example in this book.

Just as values are fluid, they may remain with us for the entirety of our lives. You probably haven't guessed it from reading this book, but one of my core values is humour. Barring some sort of unforeseeable event that removes my ability to laugh and find things funny, I predict humour to be a value of mine until my dying breath. We will all have values such as these that we consider to be entrenched in our personalities, so unshakeable, that we couldn't live without them. Perhaps it is time to reflect on these values, and consider how and why they are such an integral part of our humanity.

It is important to also note what values are *not*. Values are not personality traits. Someone can be funny but their value is not "funniness;" it's more likely humour, or enjoyment. They also might be funny and not value humour at all—that's perfectly okay. Similarly, you might be a person who values wealth, but wealth isn't a value—it's a goal or ambition. Values are not the same as goals or ambitions—values *determine* what our goals and ambitions are. If you value wealth, you would likely *value* ambitiousness, or hard-work, or even greed—there are no right and wrong values, they are deeply personal and unique to everyone, and no value should be something you are ashamed of. If you value greed, I don't share this value with you—but it is no better, nor worse, than any of mine.

One of the most profound, if slightly morbid exercises to identify what our key values are, is to think about our funeral and to write our own eulogy. Outside of, and indeed, engrained within the tropes about our accomplishments and personalities, often we find the underlying and important things—our values. For example, we may write "Sheila was a lovely, warm, kind-hearted person who always put others first. She spent her life working diligently to set up her own charity, raising millions for underprivileged youth in Victoria. She always did this with a smile, a laugh, and a can-do attitude."

From this excerpt alone, we can deduce that Sheila likely valued compassion, empathy and generosity. She almost certainly valued community and optimism, selflessness and ambition. That is seven core values right there from a short excerpt of a personally written eulogy not 50 words long. But Sheila's example was easy, if not slightly unrealistic. Most of us don't set up our own charities, and certainly we don't have the capacity to raise millions for others with a kindness generally reserved for those we would consider saints. So let's try another, more realistic eulogy excerpt and see what we find value wise.

"Lynette was a quiet, reserved and deeply personal woman. She had seven children whom she raised alone after the untimely passing of her husband, Ben. Lynette worked as a florist, and every cent she earned went in to supporting her children in their educational pursuits. Though Lynette was quiet, when she did speak she was direct, purposeful and decisive with her words. She always had time for her family and close group of friends, always enjoyed her cup of coffee at her favourite local café each morning, and always had the time to tend her beloved dogs, Max and Molly."

What values can you find within this excerpt of Lynette's eulogy? You may see some that I don't, or disagree with the ones I have found. I see someone with an unshakeable sense of duty, tradition, and support. Lynette also appears to be remarkably tough—another core value. Lynette also appeared to value routine, directness, honesty and authenticity. She was hardworking and industrious. She valued education, learning, tolerance and love. Lynette, although perhaps less intriguing or even less accomplished than Sheila on paper, is a still a woman of considerable values. We all have them—even the greedy man who just accumulated possessions and made his life about work. He probably still valued security, quality and self-reliance.

I hope these exercises have given you a window into how values can be identified from a eulogy. I encourage you to now write a short eulogy for yourself, if you feel okay about it, and see what you can find.

To make things a little easier, I have provided a list of common core values below for you to peruse and identify. One little caveat about this exercise—it is far more helpful to have a list of core values that does not exceed 5-10. While it can be difficult, I encourage you to be somewhat ruthless in your quelling of values, and really spend time reflecting on values that are crucial and fundamental to who you are. I myself may have 50 values that I can identify on a whim—but only 7 I have written down that I think about when behaving. I wish you all the best on your journey of value identification—it truly will help guide, motivate and inspire you to become the person you want to be. Remember, values = meaning and purpose.

COMMON CORE VALUES CHECKLIST

- Acceptance
- Accomplishment
- Accountability
- Adaptability
- Altruism
- Assertiveness
- Attentiveness
- Balance
- Boldness
- Bravery
- Calmness
- Cleanliness
- Cleverness
- Comfort
- Commitment
- Common sense
- Communication
- Community
- Compassion
- Competence
- Confidence
- Connection
- Contribution

- Conviction
- Courage
- Courtesy
- Creativity
- Curiosity
- Decisiveness
- Dependability
- Determination
- Development
- Devotion
- Dignity
- Discipline
- Drive
- Efficiency
- Empathy
- Endurance
- Enjoyment
- Enthusiasm
- Equality
- Ethicalness
- Excellence
- Expressiveness
- Fairness
- Famousness
- Fearlessness

- Ferociousness
- Fidelity
- Focus
- Fortitude
- Freedom
- Fun
- Generosity
- Giving
- Grace
- Gratitude
- Growth
- Hard work
- Harmony
- Health
- Honesty
- Honour
- Hopefulness
- Humility
- Humour
- Imagination
- Independence
- Individuality
- Innovativeness
- Inquisitiveness
- Integrity

- Intelligence
- Joyfulness
- Justice
- Kindness
- Knowledge
- Leadership
- Learning
- Liberty
- Logic
- Love
- Loyalty
- Maturity
- Meaning
- Mindfulness
- Openness
- Optimism
- Order
- Organisation
- Originality
- Passion
- Patience
- Peace
- Performance
- Persistence
- Playfulness

- Poise
- Power
- Presence
- Productivity
- Professionalism
- Prosperity
- Purpose
- Quality
- Realistic
- Reasoning
- Recognition
- Recreation
- Reflectiveness
- Respect
- Responsibility
- Restraint
- Rigor
- Risk
- Satisfaction
- Security
- Self-reliance
- Selflessness
- Sensitivity
- Serenity
- Service

- Sharing
- Silence
- Simplicity
- Sincerity
- Skilfulness
- Spirituality
- Spontaneousness
- Stability
- Status
- Strength
- Structure
- Support
- Sustainability
- Talent
- Teamwork
- Thankfulness
- Thoughtfulness
- Timeliness
- Tolerance
- Toughness
- Tradition
- Transparency
- Trust
- Understanding
- Uniqueness

Val-U-es

- Unity
- Valour
- Victory
- Vision
- Vitality
- Wisdom
- Wonder

12

PROCRASTINATION

Procrastination—scourge of even the most disciplined and motivated, an unavoidable reality for most and a mysterious force driven by fear, dread and anxiety. Chronic procrastinators report greater feelings of stress than their low-procrastinator counterparts, in addition to higher incidents of illness, poorer grades, and considerably lower self-esteem (presumably stemming from greater rates of self-bullying and self-deprecation). Procrastination is the capital city of our nation named Mindlessness!

In our evolving world driven, in large part, by technological advancements in the information and entertainment realm, procrastination has become much more prevalent. Procrastination is certainly not new—but in our new, vibrant and stimulating environments, it has become much easier. You might be asking the question now—but *why* do I procrastinate? The answer is not so simple, but psychologists conjecture that procrastination is both an avoidance strategy informed by anxiety, and also in part due to our desire to want to instantly gratify ourselves (an outdated survival mechanism, much like anxiety). Instant gratification has become so easy nowadays, that we're often caught in the unhealthy and damaging cycle of thinking short term reward > long term contentment. We see it everywhere these days, and certainly with the advancements in technology, we are in many cases exploited and manipulated into seeking out instant gratification for the benefit of free market advertisers who are all vying for our time and attention. Remember: if we are using, but not paying for a product (social media, for example)—*we* generally *are* the products.

Increases in entertainment and stimulation has come at the price of a reduced ability to be productive. This is, in part, due to the fact that humans are underutilising their cognitive abilities more than ever before, due to a surge in automated technological advancements. Put simply—our devices can now do things to much greater effect, and much faster, than our hands and fingers can. This is not inherently bad—but like anything, it comes at a price. The price, in this instance, is a greater reliance on technology at the cost of our innovative brain capacities. Tasks and activities that we used to do manually, tasks that took blood, sweat and tears, are now partially or fully automated, and completed in increasingly shorter amounts of time and with considerably less effort.

Think of the classic photo album owned by our parents and grandparents. The process of creating one was innately creative and carefully curated by emotional processes, logistical thought, and informed by different contextual circumstances.

The first step was to load the camera manually with a film purchased not online, but at the local photography/print shop. We'd then carefully identify our moments to capture our photographs, based on lighting, or how our subjects were positioned, our how likely these photos were to represent how we were feeling at the time; or one of a million other reasons not related to simple convenience.

Once our camera roll was complete, which was typically at around 20-30 photos (meaning we had to be deliberate and concise with our photo taking) we'd then take the camera roll to a photo developing business, wait a day or so, before being presented with our developed photos in a neat little envelope. Not all of our photos would turn out great, but that was to be expected. Then, we'd begin to glue our photos in our albums, careful to tell a story, generally by handwriting lovely headings which communicate to future generations the when, what, why, how and who of our experiences. It might shock you to learn that this was the default and atypical process of photography not even 15 years ago!

Nowadays? This whole process is completely impractical. I can take 500 photos in a single day quite easily on my smart phone, delete any photographs that don't turn out well, add filters to make them all reasonably professional, upload them to the cloud where they'll remain forever, and create a virtual photo album with even the most basic of computer skills that would easily blow any traditional photo album out of the water.

Procrastination is certainly not caused by technology, but rather is a highly complex avoidance strategy utilised to strategically manage deeply personal and unique anxieties. Procrastination is also not abnormal—it is perfectly understandable to seek out entertaining or informative stimulation over tackling what is needed to be done; most of which is menial, boring, or as a I mentioned earlier, anxiety-provoking, or a combination of all three.

It is estimated that a whopping 80% of people procrastinate on things they need to do, with close to 100% of those procrastinators favouring some sort of technological stimulation over other means of procrastinating (exercising, reading, cleaning, socialising etc.) What this ultimately communicates is that a) procrastination is pervasive and b) anything technological is the most preferred method in which to procrastinate.

GAAP

One of the best and most effective ways to reduce instances of procrastination is to GAAP: set **Goals** (short and long-term), remain **Aware** of our preferred methods of procrastination, hold ourselves **Accountable**, and **Plan** for decisive action.

Let's put the GAAP principle into action, imagining if you will that you have three weeks to complete a very important assessment for work/educational purposes. The assessment is 3000 words long, and you estimate that this will take you approximately 20 hours to complete in total.

Let's start at the top with our short-term Goals. These will of course be deeply personal to you, but let's infer that our short-term goals are to:

- Work on our assessment for two hours on our available days
- Complete the assessment in a timely manner with as little stress, anxiety and sleepless nights as possible
- Gain knowledge and/or workable skills based on the assessment protocols
- Produce high quality work
- Write these short-term goals down somewhere. Familiarise yourself with them. Become intimate with the reasons behind *why* it is important to complete this assessment according to your short-term goals. This will be extremely important if or when you

procrastinate, when you're feeling the drop-sweat panic creeping in, or when you lose sight of why you're even bothering with this "stupid assessment!"

Next, consider your long-term goals in regards to this assessment. Again, these will be deeply personal, but let's assume:

- This assessment will give me valuable knowledge that I'll be able to use in my career going forward
- This assessment will help me learn valuable research and communication skills I can use in any field
- It is important to me that I am well educated, disciplined, and hard-working
- I value learning

We can see that there is a sense of meaning, purpose, and value-driven action embedded in these long-term goals. While short-term goals are crucial in keeping us disciplined and motivated, it is equally important to reflect on the larger, more philosophical and meaning-imbued reasons behind why this assessment is going to improve our lives, or make us a better person, or increase feelings of fulfilment.

Let's move on now to the first A in GAAP—remaining Aware of our preferred methods of procrastination. How often have you been focused on an important piece of work, to find yourself in a trance-like hypnotic state scrolling through social media with absolutely no concept of when we began this process? We've all been there, and this testifies to the mindlessness that is increasingly apparent in modern society. What we lack in this scenario is mindfulness (present moment awareness), that is absolutely vital in combating these unfortunate instances of mindlessness. In order to contravene this damaging cycle, while focused on our incredibly important assessment with a three-week due date, it is absolutely crucial to identify the ways in which we prefer to procrastinate. Typically, the main instigators of procrastination are as follows:

- The internet
- Smart phones
- Social media
- Email
- Pornography
- Social invitations
- Television
- Other important projects

Only through gradual awareness of what makes us unaware, can we gradually become more aware of what makes us unaware so we can increase our awareness. Let's break this confusing and frustrating cycle!

The second A in GAAP—accountability—is another important step in overcoming the damaging cycle of persistent procrastination. This step is closely aligned with awareness, since we need to be aware of what we have engaged in procrastination-wise, in order to be able to hold ourselves accountable for where we can improve. Typically speaking, there are four different identified types of procrastinators:

- The Performer—"I work best under pressure!"
- The Self-Deprecator—"I'm dumb stupid and lazy"
- The Busy-Body—"I literally don't have the time to study"
- The Novelty-Seeker—"I'm going to write a new song instead!"

You may be one, or all of the above procrastinators naturally, or at different times depending on the task in front of you. I have personally been all of these (and more) during the process of writing this book!

Being aware, and then firmly (but gently) pointing out to ourselves where we have strayed from our existing goals are all crucial elements to reducing our procrastination.

Accountability is a natural progression from goal-setting and awareness, since it involves a persistent *reflection* of our goals "I will work on my assessment for one hour before going on social media" and a *deflection* of our procrastination habits "I haven't even worked on my assessment for ten minutes yet, I will *not* go on social media until the time is up!"

Lastly, we arrive at our P—to Plan. We are all *very* different types of planners and organisers, so I will refrain from advising you *how* plan, but rather communicate *why* planning is so important in our journey to reduced procrastination. Planning will inevitably involve elements of Goal-identification, Awareness and Accountability, thus taking the GAAP acronym full-circle. Your planning may look more rigid and structured "I will work between the hours of 11am and 3pm on my assessment today, with a 45 minute break for lunch," or more fluid and circumstantial "my dinner plans have been cancelled for Friday, I'm going to work on my assessment instead," or a mix of both.

You may be a very ordered type of person who schedules in the time to study systematically, or a more flexible person who zigs and zags when opportunities are presented to you. You might have a preconceived notion of who the better planner might be out of these two individuals—yet both of these types of people can be effective planners in the right circumstances, and both can be master procrastinators who fail to get anything done. Allow me to demonstrate using examples from two of my friends—who I'll name Mr. Systematic, and Ms. Flexible.

Mr. Systemic is a terrific organiser. He will organise his times to study in a diary, get everything prepared and structured and laid out, preparing his two hours well in advance to "smash" his study. He then spends his entire two-hour study block looking at YouTube and Reddit, and is then completely distressed because he has no time organised to study for another week!

Contrarily, Ms. Flexible is a terrible organiser who likes to go with the flow. She might expect to be having a brunch date with a friend at 11am on Saturday morning, only to receive a message at 10am from her friend who has to cancel due to an emerging cold. Ms. Flexible assesses the situation, seeing an opportunity to work on her assessment for a two hour window that she previously didn't have. She calls this "playing with house money" and, armed with her Goals, Awareness and Accountability, studies effectively in this time frame. As we can see - both Mr. Systemic and Ms. Flexible can be effective planners; and both individuals can be equally impressive procrastinators.

To Plan in the most efficacious way possible, you may like to ask the following questions of yourself:

- Am I more like Mr. Systemic or Ms. Flexible?
- What are my available times?
- How can I find the 20 hours needed (and possibly more) to complete my assessment?
- How can I reward myself for doing great work; how can I hold myself accountable for spending too much time on my preferred methods of procrastination?
- What environment is best for me to learn in?
- What kind of learner am I? (Visual, auditory, kinaesthetic, etc.)
- Are there any conflicts in my life right now that might affect my ability to work on my assessment?

Maximise Mindfulness, Minimise Mindlessness

- What excuses might I make for myself?
- How can I ensure I remain true to myself, yet improve on my ability to work uninterrupted by procrastination methods?

Hopefully, this chapter has given you some vital information about procrastination, and has provided you with some useful strategies to utilise mindfulness, to combat procrastination and quell instances of unhelpful mindlessness. Remember that procrastination shares a very intimate relationship with mindlessness—and the best cure for mindlessness, is mindfulness!

13

THE A WORD

Acceptance literally translates to "taking what is offered". It is often confused with "putting up with" or "being ambivalent" or "toughing it out," but it is far more intuitive a concept than that. Unfortunately, modern society often tells us to *not* accept. We are taught, often from a very young age, that we can "be whatever we want to be" (often, we absolutely can't) or that if we don't like something, we can simply change it. These are consistent messages we find in popular self-help books, even from flawed parenting strategies, and while perhaps they are intended as encouraging sentiments, they often fail to take into account the indiscriminately difficult and complex nature of life itself. They also preach trying to exert control, authority and power in situations which, as we know, we often have zero control, no sense of authority, and are left rendered powerless.

These concepts, while taught with no ill-intentions, can be incredibly damaging for people to learn and regurgitate, especially young people. What ideas like "you can manifest your own destiny" effectively communicate is that if we *cannot* change a situation we don't like, we are inherently defunct or flawed. We often feel like failures, when it is really a *failure to accept* that is the core issue. When we learn to accept that which we cannot change, learn to accept our pasts and our present without self-deprecation and self-bullying, and learn to accept our often unreasonable and impossibly tough external environments, we find greater levels of tranquillity within and a readiness to live.

If I had to define what acceptance is in my dictionary, I'd say it is the recognition of our own inherent limitations in circumstances that cannot be changed, and the concurrent realisation that

The A Word

no internal struggle or effort should therefore be exerted.

A perfect example of this is traffic. You'd be hard-pressed to find a single person who has ever been caught in traffic that hasn't been effected emotionally by it. I am so guilty of this—I often get upset, using my shoulda, woulda, couldas to try and justify the great injustices of traffic, daydreaming unrealistic scenarios to the issue in front of me—like that if I could teleport, I could avoid traffic going forward. Unfortunately, no amount of manifest destiny, or belief I can be whatever I want will make this a reality. All this does, usually, is take me out of the present moment, takes me away from mindfulness, and makes me more infuriated that not only am I caught in traffic, but I'm also not a superhero who can use his powers to avoid traffic!

Realistically speaking, what can we do about traffic? The answer is absolutely nothing. Sure, we can change our lifestyles in the future to accommodate increasing traffic (I might buy a motorcycle, or start taking the train) but returning to the present, where I am *right now*—stuck in traffic—I cannot change a thing. Of course, no one can tell me to wait patiently; I'm angry, after all.

But what must come eventually is a true acceptance over the fact that I am completely limited in my capacity to change the fact that I'm stuck in traffic. At the end of the day, for all my ranting, raving, daydreaming and future planning—the cars in front of me aren't moving, I might be late to work or some other engagement, and I can't change a damn thing about it.

Feelings of powerlessness, which are often a core component to facilitating acceptance, are understandably scary. People seldom like to feel powerless, and often feelings of powerlessness are accompanied by vulnerability, anger, sadness and a desire to turn that powerlessness into a sense of control or authority. This is when we see people in traffic beeping their horns, pointing the finger at others, not allowing others to merge—it is a desperate attempt to remain in control (by ironically losing control of one's behaviour) due to a lack of acceptance of the fact that they are, really, powerless. So, when we feel powerless, we often try to eliminate the feelings of vulnerability by attempting, often futilely, to assert control. What we should be doing, however, is the exact opposite—surrendering control.

Surrendering control is not admitting defeat. It is recognising, quite intelligently, that a situation *cannot* be changed no matter how much ranting, raving, punching, screaming, fighting, bargaining or rationalising you throw at it. It is akin to allowing your body to go limp when you fall from a raft into dangerous rapids. If we tried to assert control in that situation—attempting to grab onto rocks or swim in a certain direction—all we'd do is tense up our bodies, bash into things, injure ourselves severely and risk death. If we go limp however, remaining calm and keeping our bodies flat, we will naturally align with the direction of the water. While we may bump into a few rocks, we will generally avoid serious injury and stay afloat until we reach calmer waters.

Referring back to the traffic metaphor earlier, if we tried to assert control over the situation—the traffic still will not move. In the event where we are beeping our horns, swearing, fantasising and even fighting with other drivers, all we're effectively doing is taking ourselves out of the present moment and ruining our moods. However, if we acknowledge that the traffic is a situation we are powerless to control, and spend some time noticing our breath, our senses, our emotions, how the weather is looking, what is happening on the radio, the sounds of traffic, we will remain mindful; a little calmer, a little bit more content, a little bit more at peace. Just like falling from a raft on rapids and going limp, we are surrendering control intelligently and floating down the river with minimal injuries.

You'll notice I emphasised the phrase "a little bit" there because often, a little bit is all you need. It also, perhaps more importantly, emphasises the fact that nothing—not mindfulness, nor gratitude, nor acceptance—will be a magic fix-it-all for any life problem that arises. It takes time, effort, discomfort, and a multitude of different life-affirming activities to improve your wellbeing. In this instance, working on acceptance can be an incredibly worthwhile and useful exercise to incorporate into your daily life, but it is not the be all and end all, and I don't want you to believe that it is.

When we are faced with issues that make us feel powerless or vulnerable, and result in feelings of frustrations, irritation, sadness or rage that we cannot amend, it is always worthwhile to discern if acceptance can be applied. In any case, below is an incredibly useful mindfulness exercise that can be effectively applied in situations where acceptance is totally applicable in order to reduce stress, and increase feelings of peace and contentment. If an event occurs that *is* within your control—simply refer back to the values chapter, and think about acting in a way that is aligned with your personal values.

Please continue to the next page and employ the very simple flowchart on acceptance for something in your life you're failing to come to terms with, right now. Although it is basic, it covers mindfulness of breath, body and emotions, which are all crucial elements in the journey of acceptance. This flowchart can be used wherever you are, and can take as little as a couple of minutes to complete.

This exercise is effectively combining acceptance with mindfulness exercises on breath, body, and emotions that have already been covered in this book. You begin the process by acknowledging your powerlessness to control an event, however uncomfortable that may be, and then proceeding to focus on your breath. Remember—your breath is always there, and it is always present. Most importantly, you can *always* control your ability to focus on it—how empowering is that!?

You are then noticing your body as a preface to locating a physical sensation within your body. Your

Maximise Mindfulness, Minimise Mindlessness

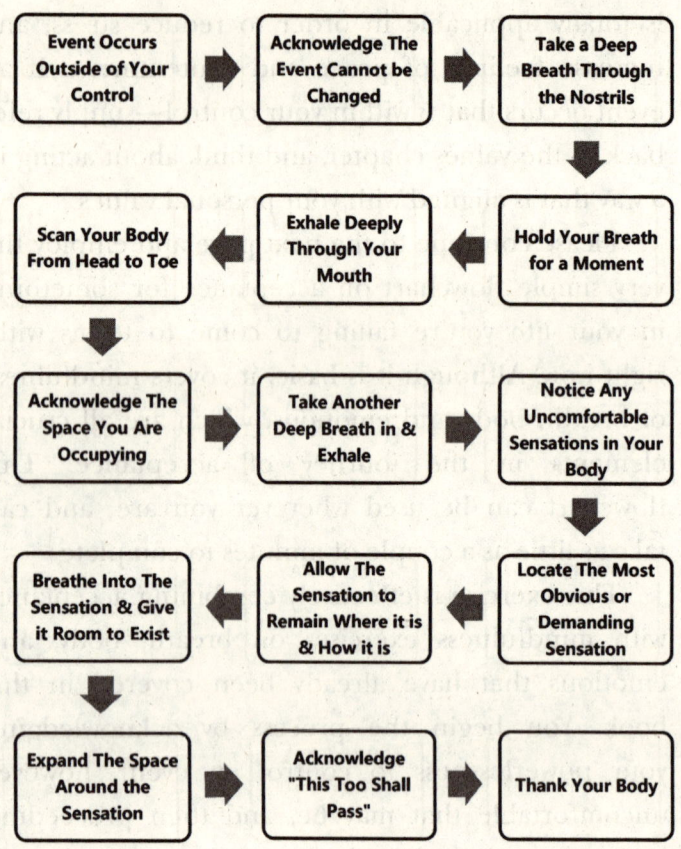

emotions always present themselves as a physical sensation, so you are simply giving yourself the time to locate the most pressing "action-requiring neurological impulse." Rather than trying to push away this emotion, or control it, you are then

The A Word

surrendering control and just allowing it to be there—however painful it may be for you (that is courage personified, well done!)

Here you are acknowledging that emotions cannot and should not be tossed aside, that they are worthy of your attention. You are then fleshing this experience out by *expanding* the space around the emotion. Rather than pushing your precious emotion away, you are actually embracing it and giving it some space to breathe. You're basically saying "I see you emotion, and I hear you. You are worthy and I'm going to give you some room to manoeuvre." Following this expansion, which will give your emotion the space it needs to process itself and eventually dissipate (most emotions last about 90 seconds) you are then acknowledging that—like every single thing that has and will ever occur in your life—this event, and this emotion, will pass. Nothing lasts forever, and you certainly don't need me to tell you that, but sometimes we completely forget this.

Finally, you are nurturing yourself. You are thanking your wonderful body for showing this emotion to you. You are thanking yourself for being courageous enough to sit with your emotions. You are thanking yourself for accepting your powerlessness, and accepting that the event is beyond your capacity to control. That not only makes you a big person with an immense capacity for self-love—it is helpful too!

14

FINAL THOUGHTS

Dear reader, thank you for taking the time to read this book. I'm so grateful for your support, your attention, and your courage.

I truly hope you gained enough from your experience in this book to increase mindfulness in your every-day life, and to simultaneously decrease the amount of mindlessness you are privy to. I just wanted to finish with some final words that are so important to hear, but rarely get spoken either by yourselves internally, or from the outside world. I am speaking from the heart, and these words can be applied to anyone. I hope that once you hear them you *will* take them to heart; but more importantly, I hope you share them with others in your life too.

You are worthy.
You deserve love.
You are capable of meaningful change.
You are enough.